奉
偷
发
明

陸
发
88/01/88

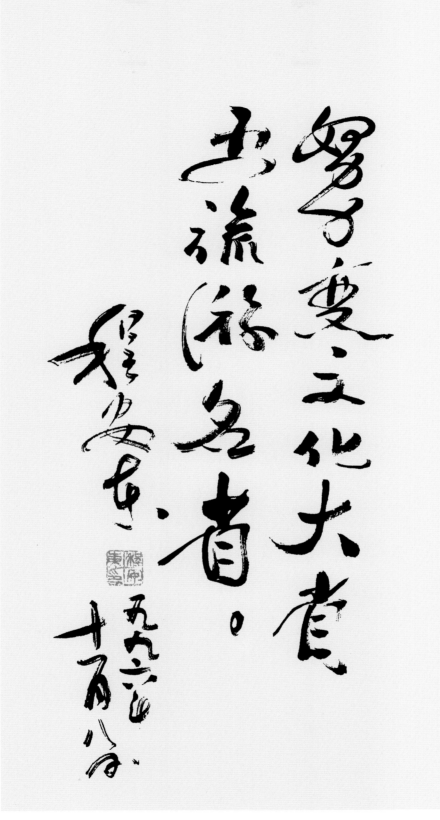

"Efforts should be made to build a famous tourist province with unique cultural features."

A dedication by Mr. Cheng An-dong, Governor of Shaanxi Province

# 陝西旅遊指南

# A GUIDE TO SHAANXI PROVINCE

主編　黑楓

Chief editor　Hei Feng

中國陝西旅遊出版社

Shannnxi Tourism Publishing House, China

# 前　言

陝西省位於中國中部偏東靠北，處在東經105°29'----110°15'、北緯31°42'----39°35'之間，總面積20.6萬平方公里，是中國的內陸省之一。按地理結構、氣候等因素，全省可劃分爲3個自然區域：北部黃土高原，中部關中平原，南部秦巴谷地。陝西以其璀璨的人文景觀、壯麗的自然景觀及濃郁的風土人情被譽爲"旅遊大省"。

這裏是中華民族文化的主要發祥地，人傑地靈，歷史上共有13個朝代在此建都，留有許多瑰麗的文化遺產，人文景觀比比皆是。

關中的西安現在還保留着周、秦、漢、隋、唐五大古都的文化遺址，被稱爲世界四大文明古都之一。因此，以西安爲中心的關中人文景觀的主要特點是周秦漢唐文化。著名景觀有秦始皇兵馬俑博物館、法門寺博物館、乾陵博物館和姜子牙釣魚臺等。

陝北歷史上曾有過突厥遷居和匈奴進犯，故部分人文景觀中留有這方面的文化印記。主要景觀有黃帝陵、鐘山石窟、二郎山廟、鎮北臺等。

陝南的漢中曾發生過蜀魏攻戰。巴蜀文化是其人文景觀的顯著特點。主要景觀有褒斜棧道、漢臺、武侯祠、武侯墓等。

陝西處於中國東南濕潤地區到西北干旱地區的過渡帶，屬大陸性氣候，由于受南北高、中間低，由西向東傾斜的復雜地勢影響，南北氣候差異較大，也孕育了一些奇特的自然景觀。

陝北黃土裸露、地貌粗獷。主要景觀有黃河壺口瀑布、毛烏素沙漠等。

陝南具有北亞熱帶氣候特色，山青水秀、風光旖旎。主要景觀有秦嶺南麓及大巴山的原始森林、榨水溶洞群等。

關中南倚秦嶺，北靠高原，介於兩者之間，主要景觀有華山、太白山、樓觀臺國家森林公園等。

由于氣候的復雜多樣性，陝西動物種類繁多。國家一級保護動物大熊貓、金絲猴、羚牛等在秦嶺南北麓均有分布。

除了文物古跡和自然風光，陝西的民風民俗也很吸引人。如陝北的腰鼓、鼙鼓、胸鼓、民間原始禮花、秧歌舞、騎毛驢迎親以及窰洞風情；關中的社火、芯子、農民畫、面花；陝南的劃龍舟、抬花轎、吊鍋、石板房、山歌等，均有一定的地域特色。

爲此，我們采用形象語言，以251幅照片爲您介紹各景點的代表性景物，供您選擇遊覽。

祝您旅遊愉快！

編者

# Foreword

Shaanxi Province, one of the landlocked areas in China, is located in the northeast part of the Midwest region, at longitudes 1050 29'-1100 15' E by latitudes 31042' - 39035'N. It covers a total area of 206,000 square kilometers. In terrain and climate, it is divided into three natural regions: the Loess Plateau in the north, the Guanzhong Plains in the middle and the Qinba Valley in the south. Shaanxi Province is universally known as a "hot travel destination" for its superb cultural heritage, tchenatural phenomena and time-honored customs.

Shaanxi Province is one of the cradles of the Chinese culture and a hotbed of outstanding people. It was intermittently established as the capital of the thirteen feudal dynasties in history. It boasts unique cultural and historical heritage.

One of the four ancient civilizations in the world, Shaanxi Province has on its vast Guanzhong Plains numerous cultural sites that have survived from such feudal dynasties as the Zhou, the Qin, the Han, the Sui and the Tang. The historical heritage on the Guanzhong Plains, with Xi'an as its center, assumes the cultural traits of these feudal dynasties. Typical examples are the Museum of the First Qin Emperor's Terra-cotta Army, Famen Temple Museum, Qianling Museum, and Jiang Tai Gong's Fishing Platform.

Historically, Shaanxi Province was once inhabited by the Turks and invaded by the Huns. As a result, part of its historical heritage bears the cultural features of the two ethnic tribes, represented by the Yellow Emperor's Mausoleum, Mount Zhongshan Grottoes, Mount Erlang Temple, and Zhenbeitai Beacon Tower.

The city of Hanzhong in southern Shaanxi witnessed one of the battles between the Wei and Shu kingdoms. Its historical heritage has close relation to the Bashu Culture, represented by Baoxie Plank Road, the Ancient Han Dynasty Platform, Wu Hou's Temple and Wu Hou'sTomb.

Shaanxi Province has a continental climate, and lies in the meeting place of two different climate types: humid and arid. Topographically, it is high in the northern and southern regions, but low in the middle, and its terrain gradually slopes from west to east. There exist vast disparities in climate between the north and the south. As a result, it has a diversity of natural landscape with unique features.

The Loess Plateau is characterized by rugged and irregular land forms. Hukou Waterfall and Mu Us Desert are examples of the kind.

Subtropical climate features, green hills, clear waters and beautiful scenery are typical of Shaanxi Province in its southern region. Its tourist attractions are the primitive forests in the southern hills of the Qinling Range and in the Dabashan Mountains, and the limestone caves in Zhashui County.

The Guanzhong region, with the Qinling Range in the south and the Loess Plateau in the north, is primarily represented by Mount Hua, Mount Taibai and Louguantai National Forest Park.

Shaanxi Province is an optimum habitat for vast numbers of wild animals because of the variety and diversity of its climate. The giant panda, the golden-haired monkey and the antelope are among the class-A state-protected animals, and they are mainly distributed in the southern hills of the Qinling Range.

In addition to its historical heritage and natural landscape, Shaanxi Province boasts distinctive and appealing folk customs, such as the waist drum dance, the breast drum dance, fireworks, the yangko dance, the bride-meeting ceremony, the dwelling cave, the raised-platform theatrical performance, the shehuo festival, the peasant painting, the steamed dough ornament, the regatta, the bridal sedan chair, the hanging pot, the stone slab house, and the mountain song.

This guidebook is intended to familiarize its readers with a well-selected array of tourist attractions particular to Shaanxi Province in vivid language and with 251 pictures. Wish you a pleasant time in Shaanxi!

Editor

# 目　　錄

# Table of Contents

# 关 中 旅 游 线 路 图 （示意）
## GUANZHONG TOUR ROUTE LINE (SKETCH)

西岳庙
XI YUE TEMPLE

华阴
HUAYIN

华山
MT·HUASHAN

秦始皇兵马俑博物馆
MUSEUM OF TERRA－COTTA
WARRIORS AND HORSES

药王山
MT·MEDICINE KING

临潼
LINTONG

华清池
HUAQING POOL

西安市
XI AN CITY

耀县
YAOXIAN

兴教寺
XING JIAO TEMPIE

长安
CHANGAN

咸阳市
XIANYANG CITY

户县
HUXIAN

乾陵博物馆
QIANLING MUSEUM

乾县
QIANXIAN

兴平
XINGPING

茂陵博物馆
MAOLING MUSEUM

楼观台森林公园
LOUGUANTAI

法门寺
FAMEN TEMPIE

杨贵妃墓
TOMB OF CONCUBINE YANG

周至
ZHOUZHI

周公庙
ZHOUGONG TEMPLE

扶风
FUFENG

马召镇
MAZHAO ZHEN

岐山
QISHAN

眉县
MEIXIAN

太白山
MT·TAIBAI

宝鸡县
BAOJI XIAN

姜子牙钓鱼台
JIANG ZI YA'S GDING
FISHING STAGE

宝鸡市
BAOJI CITY

炎帝陵
YANDI MAUSOLEUM

## 图 例  LEGEND

| | |
|---|---|
| 铁路 | RAILWAY |
| 高速公路 | EXPRESS HIGHWAY |
| 公路 | HIGHWAY |
| 景点 | SCENIC SPOT |
| 市、县、镇 | CITY COUNTY TOWN |
| 火车站 | RAILWAY STAION |
| 汽车站 | BUS STOP |

西 安 市 区 旅 游 线 路 图 （示意）

XI'AN CITY AREA TOUR ROUTE LINE (SKETCH)

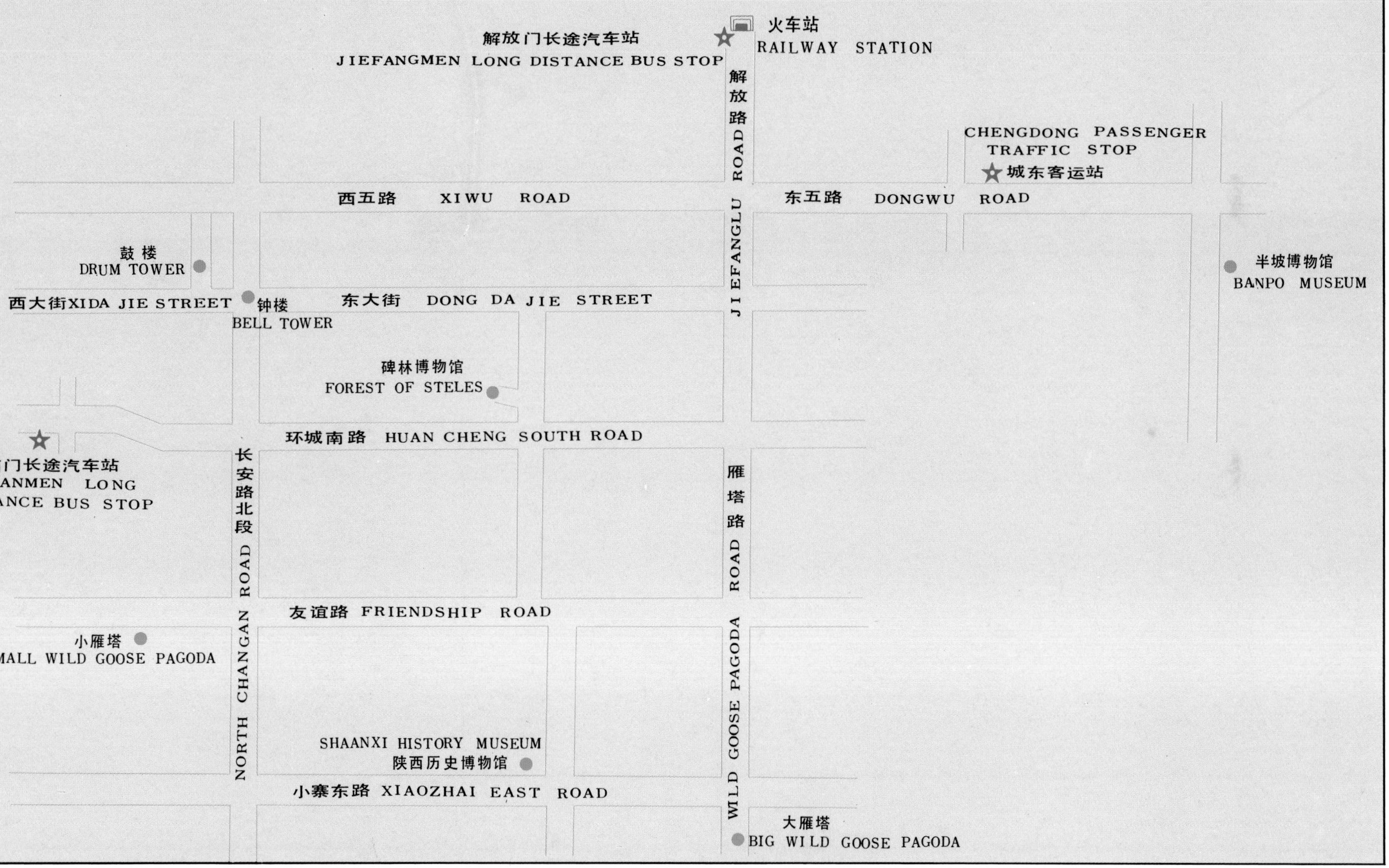

半坡博物馆 BANPO MUSEUM

城东客运站 CHENGDONG PASSENGER TRAFFIC STOP

东五路 DONGWU ROAD

火车站 RAILWAY STATION

解放路 JIEFANGLU ROAD

解放门长途汽车站 JIEFANGMEN LONG DISTANCE BUS STOP

西五路 XIWU ROAD

东大街 DONG DA JIE STREET

碑林博物馆 FOREST OF STELES

大雁塔 BIG WILD GOOSE PAGODA

雁塔路 WILD GOOSE PAGODA ROAD

鼓楼 DRUM TOWER

钟楼 BELL TOWER

西大街 XIDA JIE STREET

环城南路 HUAN CHENG SOUTH ROAD

长安路北段 NORTH CHANGAN ROAD

友谊路 FRIENDSHIP ROAD

陕西历史博物馆 SHAANXI HISTORY MUSEUM

小寨东路 XIAOZHAI EAST ROAD

小雁塔 SMALL WILD GOOSE PAGODA

小南门长途汽车站 XIAONANMEN LONG DISTANCE BUS STOP

5

# 秦 始 皇 兵 馬 俑 博 物 館
## The Museum of the First Qin Emperor's Terra-cotta Army

秦俑博物館是在秦始皇兵馬俑坑遺址上建造的大型博物館，位於臨潼縣城東5公裏處，占地約20萬平方米。已發現兵馬俑坑3個，内有與眞人眞馬大小相仿的陶俑近8000件。排列有序，步伍嚴整，車、步、騎3兵種混合編製，組成各種戰陣，充分展示了秦軍將卒的威武強大。此外，還有介紹秦陵、秦俑坑文物的輔助陳列及銅車馬陳列。

秦俑坑的發現被譽爲"世界第八大奇跡"，且被聯合國列爲世界文化遺產。

In March 1974, When Yang Zhi Fa, a peasant, digging a well, he first found some drought uncovered clay warriors, that is the Terrocotta Army.

The Museum of the First Qin Emperor's Terra-cotta Army is a large-sized museum built on the site of the First Qin Emperor's Mausoleum. The museum lies five kilometers east of the seat of Lintong County, and occupies an area of roughly 200,000 square meters. Three rectangular vaults, with 8,000 life-size pottery warriors and horses, have been discovered and unearthed. The orderly and uniform arrangement of charioteers, infantrymen and cavalrymen in various battle formations may well display the mighty power of the Qin army. In addition, there are special exhibitions on the bronze chariots and other relics unearthed from the site.

The First Qin Emperor's pottery army enjoys a reputation as the "8th world wonder", and it has been listed into the World Heritage List by the United Nations.

◀1974 年 3 月，農民楊志發在挖井時首先發現了兵馬俑。

一號坑側景
▼ A Profile of Vault No. 1

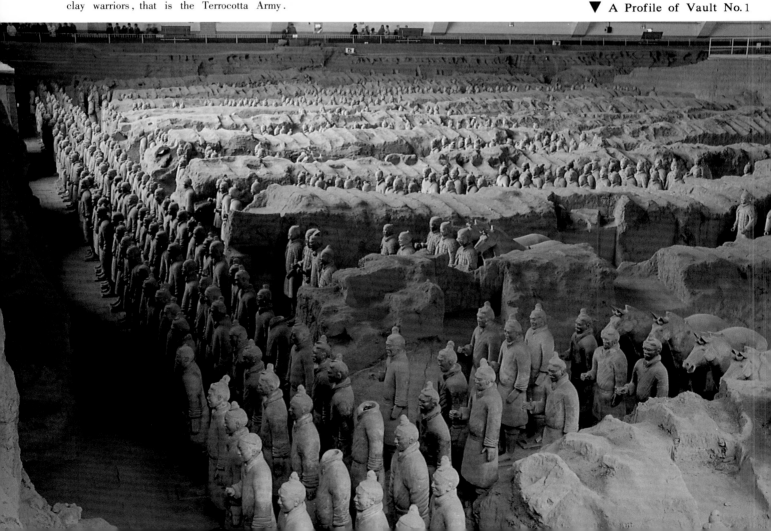

武士俑頭
▼ The Head of a Pottery Warrior

跪射俑
▼ The Kneeling Arrow Shooter

▲ 二號坑棚木遺跡　　The Site of the Wooden Shelter in Vault No. 2

一號坑全景
A Panorama of Vault No. 1

▲ 二號坑發掘現場
Newly-Earthed Site of Vault No.2

▲ 三號坑遺跡
The Site of Vault No.3

車馬兵陣
▼ A Mixed Formation of War Chariots, Horses & Infantrymen

▲ 軍陣
The Military Formation

◀ 一號坑局部
A View of Vault No. 1

# 華 山 Mt. Huashan

華山位於華陰市南，海拔最高2160.5米，以險、峻、挺拔而冠于五岳，素有"奇險天下第一山"的美譽。此山共有五峰，以南峰落雁、東峰朝陽、西峰蓮花爲主，鼎峙聳立、巍峨入雲。北峰雲台、中峰玉女各具殊姿。從山麓至絕頂，主要有千尺崠、百尺峽、蒼龍嶺、鷂子翻身、長空棧道等險道奇觀。另外還有玉泉院等道教宫觀及原始森林。是我國著名的風景名勝區。

Mount Hua, with an elevation of 2,160.5 square meters, is situated in the south of Huayin County. For its steep and perilous cliffs, it has gained a reputation as the "most precipitous mountain under heaven". It is distinctly outlined by its five prominent peaks: the Wild Goose Peak, the Sunrise Peak, the Lotus Peak, the Cloudy Peak and the Central Peak. These peaks rise aloft into the clouds. Along the only path from the hillside to the finial are the Thousand-Foot Precipice, the Hundred-Foot Previce, the Hundred-Foot the hillside to the finial are the Thousand-Foot Precipice, the Hundrde-Foot Crevice, the Blue Dragon Ridge, the Sparrow Hawk Cliff and the Cliffside Plank Road. The Yuquan Garden and the primitive forest offer a special attraction to the traveling public. Mount Hua is universally recognized as a famous tourist destination in China.

▲ 華山松
The Cypress Trees on Mount Hua

下棋亭　秦小平攝
▼ The Chess-Playing Pavilion
( Photo by Qin Xiao-ping)

西　峰
The West Peak

蒼龍嶺
▼ The Blue Dragon Ridge

長空棧道
▼ The Cliffside Plank Road

▲ 南天門勝境
A Spectacular View of the
Nantianmen Gate

三公山
▼ Mount Sangong

◀ 通向西峰的山脊
The Ridge Leading to the West Peak

# 西嶽廟 Xiyue Temple

西嶽廟位於華陰市,南距華山7公里,是歷代帝王祭謁華山神少昊的場所及巡狩行宮。始建於漢武帝元光初年(前134年),后又多次整修,現存古跡多爲明清風格。

　　該廟是五嶽廟中唯一正對主峰的祭廟。總面積12萬多平方米,廟區整體布局嚴謹,殿宇軒昂,亭廊古朴,松柏參天,碑石林立,高垣圍繞,是一座重城式建築,素有"小故宮"之譽,以其規模之大號稱"五嶽第一廟"。

　　這裏自然環境幽雅,人文景觀薈萃,是全國重點文物保護單位。

Xiyue Temple, which is situated in Huayin County, seven kilometers south of Mount Hua, began to be built in the first year (314 B.C.) of Emperor Wu Di's Yuanguang reign. The temple was initially constructed in the honor of Shao Hao, the god of Mount Hua, but later served the imperial rulers as a resort palace. Over the past few years, much repair and maintenance work has been conducted on it with great success. Most of its monuments date back to the Ming and Qing dynasties.

The temple is the only one of the mountain-based temples in China that stands opposite the main peak at a distance. It covers an area of 120,000 square meters. This ritual place has a well-planned architectural structure within its precincts, completewith imposing halls, old pavilions, tall pines and cypresses, and stone tablets. The temple is known as a small "Imperial Palace", and as the largest of its kind among the top five mountains of China.

With a superb environment and an array of cultural heritage, the temple is a class-A historical monument under the state protection.

▲ 古柏和少昊之都牌坊
The Old Cypresses & the Arch way for the God of Mount Hua

廟内景色
▼ A View of the Temple

▼ 灝靈殿　The Great Spirit Hall

▲ 乾隆御碑
The Stone Tablet with Emperor
Qian Long's Inscriptions

▲ 宋陳搏楹聯碑
The Stone Tablets with Chen Bo's Inscriptions 17

▲ 唐玄宗御製華山銘殘碑　　The Monument to Mount Hua by Emperor Xuan Zong

# 華清池 Huaqing Pool

華清池位於臨潼縣城南的驪山腳下。因此地靠驪山、多溫泉，故自周幽王修驪宮始，秦始皇、漢武帝、唐太宗、唐玄宗均在此修宮建院，玄宗時達至高潮并建"蓮花湯"、"芙蓉湯"與楊貴妃沐浴。現主要景物有飛霜殿、沉香殿、九龍湯、飛虹橋、九龍湖、九曲迴廊、五間廳和"兵諫亭"。此處亭臺樓閣遙相呼應，山光水色異常秀美。每逢夕陽西下，霞映山巒，青山披金，格外妖嬈。關中八景中之"驪山晚照"即源於此。華清池是國家重點文物保護單位。

Huaqing Pool lies at the foot of Lishan Mountain south of Lintong County. Historically, King You of the Western Zhou Dynasty ordered the construction of a resort palace for His Majesty on the site ---- an example for Emperor Qin Shi Huang of the Qing Dynasty, Emperor Wu Di of the Han Dynasty, and Emperor Tao Zong and Emperor Xuan Zong of the Tang Dynasty. But the climax occurred in Emperor Xuan Zong's reign of the Tang Dynasty, thus bringing the Lotus Flower Pond and the Chinese Flow into completion.

Among its major attractions are the Frost Drifting Hall, the Agalloch Eaglewood Hall, the Nine-Dragon Pool, the Hovering Rainbow Bridge, the Nine-Dragon Lake, the Nine-Bend Corridor, the Five-Room Hall, and the Remonstration Pavilion. Its halls and pavilions are symmetrically distributed; its natural scenery is unique and beautiful. The mountain waves, when bathed in a myriad of golden rays at sunset, are an exceptional attraction to the visiting public. One of the first eight scenic spots across thanzhong Plains is located in the area of Huaqing Pool, known as the "Lishan Mountain in Evening Sun Rays". It is now a class-A historical monument under the state protection.

華清池景致
▼ Huaqing Pool 1.  A View of Huaqing Pool

▲ 園中亭榭
The Pavilions in Huaqing Pool

◀ 飛虹橋
The Hovering Rainbow Bridge

▲ 飛霜殿及配殿　　The Flying Frost Hall & its Side Halls

# 西安半坡博物館　Xi'an Banpo Museum

半坡博物館位於西安市東郊的半坡村，是6000年前典型的母系原始氏族公社的聚居村落遺址。總面積達5公頃，其中有生活區、製造區和埋葬區3個主要部分。發掘面積約1公頃，出土有大量的"仰韶文化"時期房屋遺址、圈欄遺址、陶窯遺址、生產和生活用具、墓葬等文物。是國家重點文物保護單位。

Xi'an Banpo Museum, which is located in Banpo Village on the eastern outskirts of Xi'an, houses the archaeological site of a typical matriarchal clan community village that existed some 6,000 years ago. It covers a total area of five hectares, and comprises the living section, the working section and the burial section. The site under excavation is approximately one hectare in size. What was discovered on the site dates back to the period of Yangshao Culture, including primitive houses, pig sties, ttery kilns, production tools, daily utensils and burial objects. The museum is now a class-A historical monument under the state protection.

◄ 小孩甕棺群
A Collection of Burial Jars for the Dead Infants

博物館正門
▼ The Front Gate to the Museum

▲ 雙連灶
The Connected Fire Chamber

袋狀窖穴
▼ The Bag-shaped Storage Pit

▼ 三層迭壓房屋遺跡　　The Site of the 3-layred House

▲ 圈欄及周圍小溝　The Pigsty and the Dividing Ditch

# 西安城牆　Xi'an City Wall

西安城牆是明洪武三年（公元1370年）在唐皇城基礎上擴建而成的。矩形城池牆體總長13.74公里，高10－12米，頂寬12－15米，底厚15－18米。牆外包磚，每隔120米有一座"敵臺"，上面有屯兵敵樓。城四隅各建角樓一座，城四垣各建城門一座。每座城門都有閘樓、箭樓、正樓。箭樓與正樓之間爲甕城。環城還修有護城河。是世界上現存最大的一座較完整的古城垣。爲國家重點文物保護單位。

Xi'an City Wall was built as part of the extension work on the Imperal City in the third year (1370) of the Hongwu reign of the Ming Dynasty. The wall is rectangular in shape, with a circumference of 13.74 kilometers. It is 10 to 12 meters in height, 12 to 15 meters in width at the top, and 15 to 18 meters across at the bottom. On both sides, it was veneered with bricks. There is a rampart every other 120 meters, with a sentry building at its top. There is a watch tower on each of its four corners and a gateway on each of its four sides. Each gate is complete with a watch tower, an arrow tower and a central tower. There is an enceinte for stationing troops between the central tower and the arrow tower. Besides, there is a moat flowing around. The city wall is the most sizable and best preserved ancient wall in the world, and it is now a class-A historical monument under the state protection.

▲ 東城門箭樓
The Arrow Tower on the East Gate

▼ 北城門　The North Gate Tower

▲ 城牆、敵樓及護城河　The City Wall, the Ramparts and the Moat

城牆西南角
The Southwest Corner of the City Wall

大雁塔位於西安市城南的慈恩寺內。唐永徽三年(公元652年)，該寺主持僧玄奘爲存放從印度帶回的經書和佛像，在唐王朝允准資助下所建。武則天長安年間（公元701－704年）更折重建至今。塔高64米，7層，底邊長25米，座邊長45米。是佛教建築藝術的傑作，也是我國樓閣式磚塔的典型。爲國家重點文物保護單位。

# 大 雁 塔

## The Wild Goose Pagod

The Wild Goose Pagoda is located within the Da Ci'en Temple in the southern suburbs of Xi'an. With the financial assistance from the imperial government of the Tang Dynasty, it was built in the third year (652 A.D.) of the Yonghui reign, for storing the Buddhist classics and portraits that Master Xuan Zang had brought back from India. During the Chang'an reign (701-704) of Empress Wu Zetian, repair and maintenance work was conducted on the monument. This seven-story pagoda is 64 meters in height, and 25 by 45 meters at the foundation base. It is a masterpiece of Buddhist art and a typical wood-and-brick tower structure in China. The pagoda is now a class-A historical monument under the state protection.

# 小 雁 塔

## The Small Wild Goose Pagoda

小雁塔位於西安市南的薦福寺內，建於唐景龍元年(公元707年)。爲密檐式磚結構建築，原高15層，因地震坍塌了2層，現存13層，高43.3米。寺內有大鐵鐘一口，鐘聲嘹亮，"長安八景"的"雁塔晨鐘"即指此而言。是國家重點文物保護單位。

The Small Wild Goose Pagoda, which is located in the Jianfu Temple in the southern suburbs of Xi'an, was built in the first year(707) of the Jinglong reign of the Tang Dynasty. It is a multiple-eave brick structure. It originally consisted of 15 stories. The top two stories collapsed during an earthquake. The remaining part has a height of 43.3 meters. There is a huge iron bell inside the pagoda, which can produce crisp and loud sounds when beaten. One of the top eight scenic spots across the Guang zhong Plains, known as the Morning Bell Sounds, is located on the very site. The pagoda is now a class-A historical monument under the state protection.

# 陝西歷史博物館    Shaanxi History Museum

陝西歷史博物館是中國第一座擁有現代化設備的大型博物館，座落在西安小寨東路。館區建築面積60000平方米，爲"中央殿堂、四隅崇樓"的仿唐建築群，呈"軸線對稱"格局。館藏文物370000多件，被譽爲"華夏寶庫"，是世界上重要的博物館之一。

展廳面積有11000多平方米，展出文物精品共3000件。基本陳列廳常設"陝西古代史陳列"，專題展廳爲"陝西青銅器珍品展"和"陝西歷代陶俑精華展"臨時展廳經常舉辦國內外高水平高層次的展覽。遊客在此可充分領略燦爛的中國古代文化。

Shaanxi History Museum, the first of its kind in China with a complete range of modern facilities, is located on the East Xiaozhai Road in the city of Xi'an. It has a total floor space of 600,000 square meters. This modern architectural complex follows the style of the Tang Dynasty, with a main building in the center and a satellite one in each of its four corners. The entire complex was symmetrically laid out. With more than 370,000 articles of historical value, the museum is highly praisedae treasure trove of the nation and as one of the most important museums in the world.

The Main Exhibition Hall, with an area of more than 11,000 square meters, displays 3,000 articles of historical value. Besides, there are a permanent exhibition hall on the "Ancient History of Shaanxi Province", a special exhibition hall for the locally-unearthed bronze objects, and a temporary exhibition hall for high-level archeological finds from around the world. The museum provides its visitors with a full understanding of the splendid Chinese culture.

▲ 歷史博物館正門
The Front Gate to the Museum

▲ 漢・兵馬俑　The Pottery Horses & Warriors ( Han Dynasty)

◀ 明・儀仗俑群　The Pottery Guards of Honor ( Ming Dynasty)

▲ 唐・"絲路使者"壁畫
The Tang- dynasty Fresco: Envoys on the Silk Road

◀ 唐・彩繪女立俑
The Painted Pottery Figurine (Tang Dynasty)

▲ 唐・馬球圖"壁畫　　The Tang-dynasty Fresco: Polo Playing

# 西安碑林博物館 Xi'an Tablets Forest Museum

碑林博物館位於西安城內三學街。北宋元祐五年（公元1090年）爲保存唐"開成石經"而建，後經各代修葺擴建，現已有6個陳列室、5個遊廊和1個碑亭。內藏有漢代以來的各種碑石墓誌1700多種，2300餘通。這裏有王羲之、虞世南、褚遂良、歐陽詢、顏真卿、柳公權、張旭等古代著名書法家篆、隷、楷、行、草各種字體的原刻碑石。是我國最大的石質書庫和書法藝術寶庫，也是我國藏碑最多的地方。爲國家重點文物保護單位。

Xi'an Tablets Forest Museum, which is located on the Sanxue Street in the urban district of Xi'an, was initially built in the fifth year (1090) of the Yuanyou reign of the Northern Song Dynasty, for storing the Classic on Filial Piety that dates back to the Tang Dynasty. Repair and maintenance work on it was conducted in the ensuing dynasties respectively. The museum consists of six exhibition halls, five verandas and a tablet pavilion. It houses more than 2,300 inscribed and memorial tablets, which fall under 1,700 varieties. The stone tablets bear the original inscriptions of such famous calligraphers as Wang Xi-zhi, Yu Shi-nan, Chu Sui-liang, Ouyang Xu, Yan Zhen-qing, Liu Gong-quan and Zhang Xu seal character, the official script, the regular script, the running hand and the cursive hand. The museum is the largest and the most voluminous library of stone works in China. It is n ow a class-A historical monument under the state protection

拴馬椿
▼ The Hitching Post

太和元氣坊和泮池
▼ The Harmony & Vitality Archway and the Semi-lunar Pond

小孩石棺
The Stone Coffin for the Deceased Infant

▲ 石刻陳列室
　 The Exhibition Hall on Stone Carvings

　 林蔭深處的碑亭
▼ The Stone Tablet Pavilion in Deep Shade

# 西安鐘樓　The Bell Tower

鐘樓位於西安市中心。明洪武十七年（公元1384年）爲保存"景雲鐘"而建，原址在今北廣濟街口，與鼓樓東西對峙，明萬曆十年（公元1582年）遷建於此。鐘樓基座呈正方形，高8.6米，面積1260.25平方米。由地平至樓頂通高36米。樓分兩層，雕樑畫棟，金碧輝煌。重檐三層，樓檐四角如鳳展翅。琉璃瓦覆蓋的攢頂上金色的寶頂分外耀目。是省重點文物保護單位。

The Bell Tower, which is located in the center of Xi'an, was built for storing the Jingyun Bell in the 17th year of the Hongwu reign of the Ming Dynasty. Initially, it stood at the entrance to the North Guangji Street, opposite the Drum Tower. The 10th year (1582) of the Wanli reign witnessed its relocation to the present-day site. Its foundation is square in shape, 8.6 meters ins height, and 1,260.25 square meters in size. This two-section tower is 36 meters from the ground level to the finial. Ita triple-eave structure with carved beams and painted rafters. Its four corners jut out as if a bird would spread its wings for a flight. Its roof, decorated with glazed tiles, looks very brilliant and imposing. The Bell Tower is now a class-A histori camonument under the provincial protection.

# 西安鼓樓 The Drum Tower

鼓樓位於西大街，建於明洪武十三年（公元1380年）。相傳明、清時樓上置鼓，擊鼓報時，故稱鼓樓。鼓樓基座呈長方形，東西長52米，南北寬37米，高7米，面積1924平方米。從地平至樓頂通高34米。樓分兩層，重檐三層，正面七開間，進深爲三間，四周有迴廊，共九個隔間。樓頂爲歇山式，貼金彩繪，金碧輝煌。是省重點文物保護單位。

The Drum Tower, which is located on the West Main Street, was built in the 13th year (1380) of the Hongwu reign of the Mings Dynasty. The tower was orignally used to store a drum in the Ming and Qing dynasties, primarily for the time-telling purpose. Its base is rectangular in shape, 7 meters in height, 52 meters from east to west and 37 meters from north to south. It covers an area of 1,924 square meters. The tower is 34 meters from the ground level to the finial. It consists of two stories inside, but has a triple-eave appearance. It has seven rooms outside and three rooms inside. There exists a covered corridor on each of its four sides. The roof of the tower, built with glazed tiles, slopes down multiple tiers of eaves. The Drum Tower is now a class-A historical monument under the provincial protection.

# 興 教 寺　Xingjiao Temple

興教寺位於長安少陵原畔，是"樊川八大寺院"之首。唐總章二年(公元669年)，爲遷葬唐代高僧玄奘遺骨而建，因唐肅宗題寺內塔額"興教"二字而得名。寺院大雄寶殿前有鐘、鼓樓對峙，內有釋迦佛鎏金銅像；藏經樓收藏了唐人手抄和近代影印的佛經數千冊；塔院內矗立着玄奘舍利塔和圓測、窺基塔。是國家重點文物保護單位。

Xingjiao Temple, situated on the Shaoling Tableland of Chang'an County, was one of the eight famous Buddhist temples in ancient times. In the second year (669) of the Zongzhang reign of the Tang Dynasty, it was built as a second burial place for Master Xuan Zang. The upper part of his stupa was horizontally inscribed with the two Chinese characters "Xing Jiao" (Rejuvenating Buddhism ) originally written by Emperor Li Heng. Hence, the name Xingjiao Temple. In front of the Great Buddhist Hall that houses a gilded bronze statue of Sakyamuni, the Bell Tower stands opposite the Drum Tower. The Chamber of Buddhist Texts houses Tang-dynosty manuscripts and modern reproductions in thousands of copies. Within the in honor of Xuan Zang, Yuan Ce and Kui Ji respectively. Xingjiao Temple is now a historical monument under the priority protection of the state government.

▲ 玄奘負笈像
**A Portrait of Master Xuan Zang with a Load of Books**

玄奘舍利塔
▼ **Master Xuan Zang's Stupa**

▲ 48臂觀音塑像　A Statue of the Goddess of Mercy with Forty-eight Arms

▼ 臥佛大殿　　The Great Hall for the Sleeping Buddha

▲ 寺内景色　　A Panorama of Xingjiao Temple

# 樓觀臺國家森林公園
## Louguantai National Forest Park

樓觀臺國家森林公園位於周至縣城東南約18公里處的秦嶺北麓。海拔507－2992米，總面積2.7萬公頃。

公園植物垂直帶譜明顯,有"40里峽"景觀、31種國家一、二級保護植物、"百花園"、世界緯度最高的"百竹園"及200公頃的竹林基地。森林縱深棲息着國家一級保護動物大熊貓、金絲猴、羚牛和其它珍禽異獸。樓觀臺道觀是中國最早的道觀,爲道教始祖、古代哲學家老子李耳講經之地。公園還有日出水量1000多噸的溫泉。

樓觀臺森林公園是人們回歸自然,進行森林浴、溫泉浴的良好休憩之地。

Louguantai National Forest Park is located in Zhouzhi County in the northern hills of the Qinling Range. The park varies in elevation from 507 to 2,992 meters, and covers an area of 2.7 hectares. The park is characterized by the vertical distribution of its vegetation. Easy access can be made to the Forty-Mile Canyon, the 30 class-A/-B plants under the state-level protection, the Hundred-Flower Garden, the world's highest-latitude baket, and the 200-hectare bamboo plantation. In the depth of the forest are living such rare animals as the giant panda, the golden-haired monkey and the takin. Louguan Temple, the first of its kind in China, was where Li Er, the philosopher, preached his religious ideas. There exists a hot spring in the park, with a daily output of more than 1,000 tons. Louguantai Forest Park, with a complete range of bathing facilities, is an excellent place for rest and relaxation.

▲ 溪水潺潺
The Babbling River

茂密的植被
▼ Dense Vegetation

▲ 羚牛
The Antelope

森林景色
▼ A Forest Scene

▲ 金絲猴
The Golden-haired Monkey

▲ 大熊貓
The Giant Panda

老子祠一角
A Partial View of Lao Zi's Temple

▲ 道觀內的翠華門
The Cuihua Gate

百竹園 The Hundred-Species Bamboo Thicket

# 藥王山　Mount Yaowang

藥王山位於耀縣城東1.5公里處。北洞景區有爲紀念隋唐時期偉大的醫學家孫思邈而建的藥王大殿以及太玄洞、醫方碑亭、洗藥池等。南庵景區是孫思邈當年的隱棲之地，有文昌閣、金代大殿、七間殿以及拜眞臺、曬藥場等遺址。此外，山上還保留着歷代碑石300餘通及隋至明代摩崖造像45尊。

Mount Yaowang is located 1 kilometer east of the seat of Yaoxian County. In the Northern Cave Scenic Zone are the Taixuan Cave, the Prescription Tablet, the Medicinal Herb Washing Pond, and the Yaowang Hall built in memory of Sun Si-miao, the great pharmacist of the Sui Dynasty. In the Nan'an Scenic Zone are located his residence, the Wenchang Mansion, the Jindai Hall, the Seven-Room Hall and the Herb Drying Yard. Besides, there are more than 300 stone tablets that have survived the ages, and 45 Ming-dynasty rock statues in the mountain.

▲ 翹檐中的柏樹
The Towering Pine Trees

▼ 藥王大殿　The Great Hall of the Great Pharmacist Sun Si-Miao

▼ 碑林　The Stone Tablet Forest

▲ 摩崖造像　The Cliffside Statues

# 茂陵博物館　Maoling Museum

茂陵爲漢武帝劉徹的墓。在興平市東。始建於公元前139年，歷時53年，所花費用佔當時每年全國稅收三分之一，是西漢帝王陵中規模最大的一座。其周圍有5座陪葬墓，霍去病墓是最大的一座，茂陵博物館現設於此，爲國家重點文物保護單位。霍去病是漢武帝手下一傑出大將，曾先后6次出征匈奴，前117年病死，年僅24歲。漢武帝令爲其重葬，并製作巨型石人、石獸16件爲墓飾。這批石刻目前保存完好，均陳列於此，其中最著名的爲"馬踏匈奴"。

Maoling Mausoleum, the final resting place for Emperor Liu Che of the Western Han Dynasty, is located east of the seat of Xingping County. The construction of the tomb started in the year of 139 B.C., and was brought into completion 53 years later. Its total expenses accounted for 1/3 of the annual state revenues. The mausoleum, the most sizable of the imperial tombs in the Western Han Dynasty, is surrounded by five satellite tombs. Huo Qu-bing's Tomb, the biggest of the satellite tombs, maration of Maoling Museum. Maoling Mausoleum is now a class-A historical monument under the state protection. Huo Qu-bing, an outstanding general under Emperor Liu Che, made six military expedition age of 24 in 117 B.C. Under Emperor Liu Che's orders, he was fully honored with sixteen stone figures and animals as burial objects in his tomb. The stone tablets are well preserved and displayed under Horse Hoofs ".

▼ 博物館内的景色
A Broad View of the Museum

▼ 西漢・馬踏匈奴石刻　　The Han-dynasty Stele: The Hun under the Horse Hoofs

▲ 霍去病墓　　The General Huo Qu-bing's Tomb

# 楊 貴 妃 墓　The Lady Yang's Tomb

楊貴妃墓在興平市西馬嵬坡前，是唐玄宗妃子楊玉環之墓。距今1200多年，墓爲磚砌，周圍回廊鑲嵌着歷代名人題詠的詩詞石刻甚多。

　　唐天寶15年（公元756年）安祿山反，6月潼關失陷，帝攜妃出奔次馬嵬驛，將士嘩變，逼帝縊妃於佛堂，死年38歲。

Lady Yang's Tomb, which is located in the periphery of Mawei Po in the city of Xingping, is the final resting place for Emperor Xuan Zong's favorite lady, Yang Yu-huan. It was veneered with blue bricks more than 1,200 years ago. In the winding corridors nearby, there are many stone tablets with the poems and prose composed by the celebrities of different dynasties.

In the 15th year (756) of Tianbao reign, An Lu-shan rose in revolt against the Tang Empire. At the news that Tongguan was occupied in June, Emperor Xuan Zong, with his favorite lady, fled to Mawei Po, where his followers mutinied, and forced Lady Yang to commit suicide in the Buddhist hall. She met with her death at the age of 38.

▲ 楊貴妃塑像
A Statue of Lady Yang

楊貴妃墓
▼ The Lady Yang's Tomb

# 法門寺　Famen Temple

**法**門寺位於扶風縣城北,有3大景點:法門寺院、法門寺博物館、東方佛都。

法門寺院內有寶塔、大雄寶殿等建築。據佛典記載,公元前272年印度阿育王為安置釋迦牟尼佛骨舍利在此建塔成寺,是中國四大佛教聖地之一。至唐代,法門寺院已成為皇家寺院。1987年對半壁坍塌的寶塔發掘時,在地宮中發現了目前世界佛教最高聖物佛指舍利(一枚靈骨、三枚影骨)及上千件唐朝供奉物。寺院現供奉着佛祖真身指骨舍利,佛事頻繁。

法門寺博物館是政府為珍藏、展覽地宮藏品而仿地宮出土的銅浮屠而建。藏品有八重寶函、鎏金四股十二環迎真身杖、皇帝御製和內庫供奉的121件(組)金銀器、女皇武則天的金蘭繡裙及上千件唐代絲金織物。另有反映佛教文化的"唐密曼荼羅"地宮、唐茶文化展室。

東方佛都的主體是一尊48米高的四面五方佛像。大佛內有"回"字型大小地宮,此外從下至上共有11層,設有反映佛教文化的"釋迦牟尼廳"、"玄奘西遊廳"、"鑒真東渡廳"和"因果報應廳"等。

法門寺現已成為集宗教,觀光為一體的佛教聖地。

## 一、法門寺院
### Famen Temple

Famen Temple is situated in Famen Town north of the seat of Fufeng County. It consists of three major parts: Famen Temple, Famen Temple Museum, and the Oriental Buddhist Center. Large-sized building structures can be seen on the premises of Famen Temple, including Famen Stupa and the Buddhist Hall. According to the historical records, the Buddhist King Asoka of ancient India had the temple and the pagoda built in 272 B.C., exclu sively for preserving the finger bones of Sakyamuni. The temple, which served the royal family in the Tang Dynasty, is now one of the most important Buddhist centers in China. In 1987 when repair Sakyamuni's four finger bones (including a real one and three shadow ones), and more than 1,000 sacrificial objects were discovered from the underground palace. The finger bones have ever since been considered the most sacred objects in the Buddhist  circ They are now enshrined and worshipped in the temple. Buddhist ceremonies are often held on the site.

Famen Temple Museum was built in the style of the bronze stupa unearthed from the underground palace, for preserving and displaying the excavated Buddhist relics, including the eight-layered chest, 121 gold and silver wares, the embroidered skirt consecrated by Empress Wu Ze-tian, and more than a thousand pieces of silk fabrics made in the Tang Dynasty. Access can also be made to the Exhibition on the Tea Culture of the Tang Dynasty and the Exhibition on the Buddhist Culture.

The Oriental Buddhist Center is dominated by a 48-meter Buddhist statue which consists of 11 stories from the bottom to the top. there are halls of all sizes inside the statue, including the Hall of Sakyamuni, the Hall of Xuan Zang's Jourmey to the west, the Hall of Jian Zhen's Voyage to Japan, and the Hasll of Casuality. Famen Temple has become a place of both religious and sighseeing activities

◀ 大雄寶殿
The Hall of Mahavira

▲ 護法韋馱菩薩
The Buddhist Guardian Sanka

◀ 釋迦牟尼佛指舍利
Sakyamuni's Finger Bones

▲ 大雄寶殿內景　　An Interior View of the Hall of Mahavira

## 二、法門寺博物館
### Famen Temple Museum

▲ 法門寺博物館景致　　A View of Famen Temple Museum

▲ "唐密曼荼羅"文化陳列宮　　The Exhibition Hall on the Buddhist Culture

▲ 唐代茶文化歷史陳列室　　The Exhibition Hall on the Tea Culture of the Tang Dynasty

鎏金盝頂四天王銀寶函
▼ The Gilded Silver Casket with the Images
of the Four Heavenly Guardians

鎏金毬路籠子
▼ The Gilded Silver Container with
Decorative Designs

▲ 鎏金捧真身銀菩薩
The Gilded Silver Buddhisattva with
Sakyamuni's Sarira

▲ 盤口細頸貼塑琉璃瓶
The Gilded & Glazed Bottle with a
Plate-shaped Mouth and a Thin Neck

55

▲ 48米高的四面五方佛像　　The 48-meter Multi-dimensional Statue of Sakyamuni

# 乾陵博物館 Qianling Museum

乾陵是唐高宗李治和女皇帝武則天的合葬陵。在乾縣城北6公里的梁山上。陵依山而鑿，規模宏大，氣勢雄偉。陵巔建有闕樓。陵下司馬道兩側對稱排列着華表、石馬、石鳥、石人、石碑等，并有61尊王賓石雕像，尤以無字碑最爲聞名。周圍的17座唐王公大臣陪葬墓已發掘5座，出土珍貴文物4300多件，壁畫100多幅。是國家重點文物保護單位。

Qianling Mausoleum, a sizable tomb shared by Emperor Gao Zong (Li Zhi) and Empress Wu Ze-tian of the Tang Dynasty, is located in the area of Liangshan Hill six kilometers north of the seat of Qianxian County. The tomb looks very imposing in the hilly setting. There stands a watch tower at the top of it. The spirit way in front of the tomb is symmetrically lined with octagonal priomatic cloud pillars, stone horses, stone birds, stone figures and stone tablets. There are also sixty-one stone statues, representing the chieftains of different minority tribes. The Wordless Monument to Empress Wu Ze-tian is the most eye-catching stone tablet in the periphery of the mausoleum. Up to date, five out of its seventeen satellite tombs have been unearthed, and more than 4,300 valuable objects and over 100 mural paintings have been discovered. Qianling Mausoleum is now a class-A historical monument under the state protection.

▲ 駝鳥石刻
The Stone Tablet with the Image of an Ostrich

▼ 唐高宗李治與武則天的合葬墓　The Joint Tomb of Emperor Gao Zong & Empress Wu Ze-tian

▲ 仕女圖（壁畫）
A Mural Painting of Waiting Maids

翼馬
▼ The Flying Horse

▲ 王賓石雕像
The Statues of Foreign Envoys and Tribal Chieftains

▲ 無字碑　The Wordless Monument to Empress Wu Ze-tian

# 太 白 山　Mount Taibai

太白山位於眉縣、周至縣和太白縣交界處，是秦嶺山脈主峰，海拔3767.2米，爲國家級自然保護區。山上原始森林茂密，珍貴的野生動植物資源豐富；第四紀冰川所"雕刻"的地貌風光——40里跑馬梁氣勢壯觀。山巓太白三池鼎列，水色蔚藍。頂峰是冰川遺跡——角峰，"太白積雪六月天"即典出於此，是古時關中著名八景之一。頂峰上的拔仙臺相傳是八大神仙聚會之處，可觀雲海日出。登山自眉縣城南的營頭鄉、周至縣的厚畛子鄉、太白縣的鸚鴿鄉均可，前者爲最佳攀登點。

Mount Taibai, the dominant peak of Qinling Range, is located where Meixian, Zhouzhi and Taibai counties meet. The mountain, with an elevation of 3,767.2 meters, is a national natural reserve covered with thick primitive forests and replete with plant and animal resources. The land forms, which were "carved" during the Quaternary Glacier Period, afford a myriad of majestic views. The same is particularly true of the 40-mile Galloping-Horse Ridge. At the top of the mountain lie three ponds with crystal-lear water, and an ever-glaciated spot known as the Corner Peak. In fact, the peak is referred to in the old saw that Mount Taibai is snow-clad under the great June heat." The snow-capped peak is on Plains. The Baxian Platform, legendarily the usual meeting place for the Eight Immortals in the traditional Chinese culture, affords a splendid view of white clouds and sunrise. Mount Taibai is accessible to the traveling public via Yingtou Town (Meixianunty), Houzhenzi Town (Zhouzhi County) or Yingge Town (Taibai County). The first route is most probably the best choice.

採藥人
▼ Medicinal Herb Diggers

太白雄姿　陳小平攝
▼ Mount Taibai in Fullest Beauty
（Photo by Chen Xiao-ping）

"淨池鳥"
The "Pure Pond Bird"

▲ 大爺海　陳小平攝
The Old Sea (Photo by Chen Xiao-ping)

太白山原始森林
▼ The Primitive forest

冰川遺跡
The Traces of the Glacier

# 周公廟　Zhougong Temple

周公廟位於岐山縣城西北7.5公里的鳳凰山南麓。三面環山，南面開闊。唐武德初年（公元618年）爲紀念西周杰出的政治家周公姬旦而建，後經歷代修葺、擴建、形成了以周三公（周公、召公、太公）殿爲主，姜嫄後稷殿爲輔，樓閣亭榭點綴其間的古建築群。整個建築布局對稱、結構精巧。廟內現存歷代碑碣30餘通，漢唐古樹多株，唐玄宗賜名的"潤德泉"一眼。玄武洞中唐代石雕"玄武像"傳說撫摸可治百病。是省重點文物保護單位和省風景名勝區

Zhougong Temple is located in the southern hill of Mount Phoenix 7.5 kilometers northwest of the seat of Qishan County. The temple, embraced by hills on three sides, was originally built in memory of Duke Ji Dan, an outstanding philosopher of the Zhou Dynasty, in the first year (618) of Wude reign of the Tang Dynasty. Repair and extension work on it was carried out in the ensuing dynasties. As a result, a well-planned building complex with halls, pavilions and towers was brought into existence. Inde the temple, there stand more than 30 stone tablets and many old trees that date back to the Han and Tang dynasties. There is also a spring in it, named the Moral Cultivation Spring by Emperor Xuan Zong of the Tang Dynasty. According to legend, the stne statue bearing "A Portrait of Tortoises" was a miraculous cure for diseases of any kind as soon as it was touched. The temple is now a class-A historical monument under the provincial protection.

▲ 周公像
A Portrait of Zhou Gong

八卦亭
▼ The Pavilion with the Eight Diagrams

64

樂樓
▼ The Music Chamber

▲ 張果老倒騎驢
Zhang Guo-lao's Way of Riding on the Donkey

碑亭
▼ The Stone Tablet Pavilion

# 姜子牙釣魚臺
## Jiang Zi-ya's Fishing Platform

釣魚臺位於寶雞縣城東南的磻溪谷中，溪中一臺石上有跪痕，相傳爲西周開國元勳姜子牙10年隱居垂釣以圖大業之地。是省重點文物保護單位和省風景名勝區。

唐貞觀年後始在此建廟並植柏4株，至今尚存。後又陸續建有18處90餘間古建築，現存多爲明清風格。主要有文王廟、太公廟、三清廟、望賢臺等。另有"璜石"、"飛瀑流霞"、"浪聲莫測"等景致。

釣魚臺南依秦嶺，北臨渭水，空氣清新，氣場特強。到此可領略姜太公隱居生活之韻味。

▲ 姜太公像
A Portrait of Jiang Zi-ya

▼ 釣魚臺　The Fishing Platform

Jiang Zi-ya's Fishing Platform is located in Panxi Vale southeast of Baoji County. A river is flowing through the vale, and by the riverside there is a stone platform with prints of knees. Legend has it that Jiang Zi-ya, one of the founders of the Western Zhou Dynasty, lived there by fishing for ten years and made plans for great ambitions. The platform is now a class-A historical monument under the provincial protection.

After the Zhenguan reign of the Tang Dynasty, temples were built in memory of Jiang Zi-ya, and pine trees were planted in them. The building complex with more than 90 partitioned rooms maintains the architectural style of the Ming and Qing dynasties. Examples include Wenwang Temple, Taigong Temple, Sanqing Temple and Wangxian Platform.

The Fishing Platform which is located between the Qinling Range and the Weihe River is permeated with fresh air and vital energy. If you pay a visit there, you will be able to experience Jiang Zi-ya's isolated life from the outside world.

▲ "璜石"　The Semi-annular Jade Pendant

▼ 姜太公廟及唐代古柏　Jiang Zi-ya's Temple & the Cypresses (Tang Dynasty)

▲ 文王廟
The Temple to King Wenwang (Zhou Dynasty)

姜子牙大戰聞太師（壁畫）
▼ The Mural Painting: Jiang Zi-ya's Victory over Wen Taishi

浪聲莫測
▼ The Unfathomable Sounds of Waves

# 炎帝陵　Emperor Yan Di's Mausoleum

炎帝神農氏是傳說中中國上古姜姓部族首領，生於今寶雞姜水之濱。他用木製作耒、耜教民生產、開創了中國的農耕文明；又嘗百草，發現葯材和教人治病，被后人崇爲始祖。

炎帝陵位於寶雞市南郊清姜河畔的常羊山上，南依秦嶺，北臨渭水。主要景點有：炎帝大殿、炎帝行宮、華夏始祖牌坊、羊脚亭、羊首亭及炎帝陵寢。

每年農曆七月初七炎帝忌日爲各界民祭活動定製。其它民間的主要祭祀有：清明祭祀、嘗新祭祀、襄災祭祀等。

Emperor Yan Di, the God of Farming in the traditional Chinese culture, is said to have served as the chieftain of a tribe whose men were surnamed Liu in the remote antiquity. He was born by the side of the Jianshui River in the present-day Baoji County. He created China's agricultural civilization by teaching his men how to farm with wooden tools and how to cure diseases with medicinal herbs. Therefore, he was revered as the Forefather by his successors.

Emperor Yan Di's Mausoleum is located on the Changyang Hill by the side of the Qingjiang River in the southern suburbs of Baoji City, with the Qinling Range in the south and the Weihe River in the north. Its major attractions are Emperor Yan Di's Great Hall, Emperor Yan Di's Resort Palace, the Memorial Hall to the Chinese Ancestor, the Yangjiao Pavilion, the Yangshou Pavilion and Emperor Yan Di's Coffin Chamber.

Grand memorial ceremonies are held to mark the anniversary of Emperor Yan Di's death on the seventh day of the 7th lunar month every year. At other times, the Qingming Festival Sacrifice, the Harvest Sacrifice, and the Sacrifice to Disaster Reduction are respectively held in the area of Emperor Yan Di's Mausoleum.

俯瞰炎帝陵
▼ A Bird's Eye View of Emperor Yan Di's Maosoleum

炎帝塑像
A Statue of Emperor Yan Di

炎帝陵寝
Emperor Yan Di's Coffin Chamber

祭祀時的表演
A Sacrificial performance

▼　祭祀情景　　A Sacrificial Ceremony

▼　祭祀情景　　A Sacrificial Ceremony

▲ 炎帝大殿及侧殿
The Great Hall of Emperor Yan Di & its Side Halls

71

# 關 中 風 情
## The Folk Customs in the Guanzhong Region

▲ 關中農村老太太
The Old Lady in the Rural Area of the Guanzhong Plains

社火隊　陳小平攝
▼ The Shehuo Performers (Photo by Chen Xiao-ping)

◄ 看社火　Watching the Shehuo Performance

▲ 民間祭品
Folk Sacrificial Offerings

▲ 掛虎臉　Wearing Tiger Masks

戲班子　陳小平攝
▼ A Theatrical Troupe（Photo by Chen Xiao-ping）

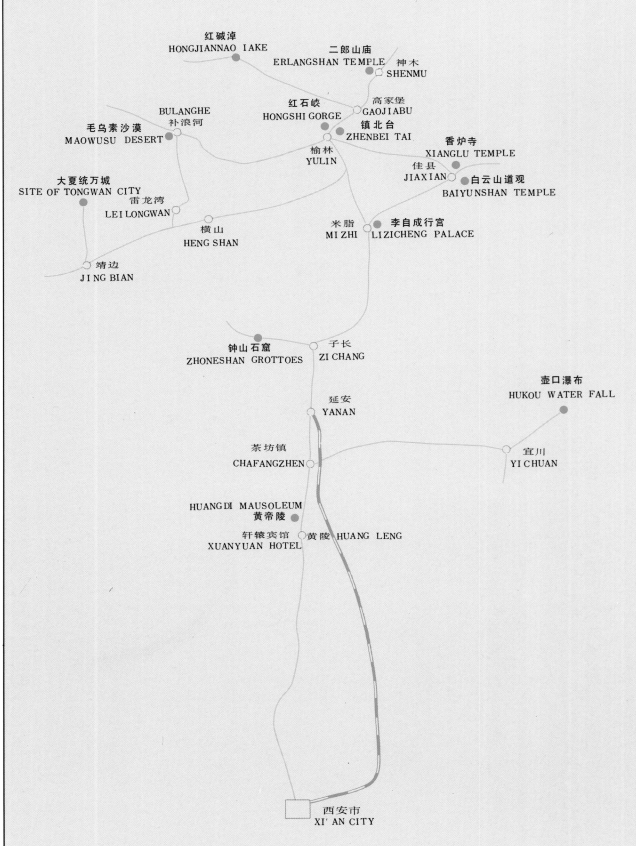

陕北旅游线路图（示意）
SHAANBEI TOUR ROUTE LINE (SKETCH)

红碱淖
HONGJIANNAO IAKE

二郎山庙
ERLANGSHAN TEMPLE

神木
SHENMU

补浪河
BULANGHE

红石峡
HONGSHI GORGE

高家堡
GAOJIABU

毛乌素沙漠
MAOWUSU DESERT

镇北台
ZHENBEI TAI

香炉寺
XIANGLU TEMPLE

榆林
YULIN

大夏统万城
SITE OF TONGWAN CITY

佳县
JIAXIAN

白云山道观
BAIYUNSHAN TEMPLE

雷龙湾
LEI LONGWAN

横山
HENG SHAN

米脂
MIZHI

李自成行宫
LIZICHENG PALACE

靖边
JING BIAN

钟山石窟
ZHONESHAN GROTTOES

子长
ZICHANG

壶口瀑布
HUKOU WATER FALL

延安
YANAN

茶坊镇
CHAFANGZHEN

宜川
YICHUAN

HUANGDI MAUSOLEUM
黄帝陵

轩辕宾馆
XUANYUAN HOTEL

黄陵 HUANG LENG

西安市
XI'AN CITY

# 黃帝陵　The Huangdi Emperor's Mausoleum

黃帝陵位於黃陵縣城北的橋山之巔。大片古柏環繞的山上有中華民族人文始祖軒轅黃帝的陵寢、祭亭；山下軒轅廟內有祭殿和下圍約10米的黃帝手植柏、黃帝的腳印石刻及歷代御製祭文石碑等諸多文物。相傳黃帝生于壽丘，長于姬水，是我國原始社會末期一位偉大的部族首領。黃帝時代曾統一了黃河流域中原地帶，形成了中華民族的雛形；完成了母系氏族向父系氏族的過渡，從此告別了野蠻時代；諸多的發明創造奠定了中華民族文化的基礎，因而受到炎黃子孫的崇仰。黃帝陵是國務院公布保護的第一號古墓葬和國家重點文物保護單位。每年清明節、重陽節均有世界各地數萬名華人、華僑雲集于此謁陵、祭祖。

陵前祭亭
▼ The Sacrificial Pavilion in Front of the Maosoleum

The Huangdi Emperor's Mausoleum is located at the top of Mount Qiaoshan north of the seat of Huangling County. The mountain is densely covered with old cypresses and pine trees. The Huangdi Emperor has long been revered and worshipped as the ancestor of the Chinese people. A temple was built in his honor. Inside the temple are the Sacrificial Hall, a thick pine tree planted by the Huangdi Emperor, a footprint-bearing slab and centuries-old stone tablmperor was born in Shouqiu, and brought up in Jishui. He was the chieftain of a tribal community in the closing years of China's primitive society. In the era of the Huangdi Emperor, the Huanghe River Valley was unified, and bec Chinese people. The era also witnessed a transition of the early social order from matriarchal to patrilineal clan communities, and put an end to the barbarous stage of the humanity. The Huangdi Emperor, a remarkable contributor to the has been much revered throughout China. The Huangdi Emperor's Mausoleum ranks first on the ancient mausoleum list published by the State Council, and stands out as a class-A historical monument under the state protection.

At the Qingming Festival and the Double Ninth Festival each year, many people of the Chinese origin the world over offer sacrifices to the Huangdi Emperor on the site of his mausoleum.

"漢武帝" 祭陵
Han Dynasty Emperor Wu
Di's Offered Sacrifices to the Yellow Emperor

▲ 軒轅黃帝像
A Portrait of the Huangdi Emperor

◄ 黃帝手植柏
The Cypress Planted by the Huangdi Emperor

各界人士祭祀盛況
The Annual Sacrificial Scene

黃帝廟門
The Huangdi Emperor's Temple

◀ 香煙裊裊
The Rising Smoke of Incense Sticks

▲ 祭祀旗隊
A Sea of Sacrificial Banners

# 鐘山石窟

## Mount Zhongshan Grottoes

鐘山石窟又稱石宮寺、萬佛洞。位於子長縣城西15公里的鐘山南麓，建於宋英治平四年（公元1067年）。洞內刻有3尊3.54米的釋迦牟尼三世佛及上萬尊神態各異、栩栩如生眾多小佛的摩崖造像，雖年深日久，但仍保留着原始彩繪顏色。石窟內外，碑碣題記甚多。現有山門牌坊、蕭寺宮、惠善法師浮圖塔、松岩法師浮圖塔、七級磚塔、禪室禪院均保存完整。是國家文物重點保護單位。

Mount Zhong Grottoes, also known as the Stone Palace Cave or the Cave for Thousands of Buddhas, are located on the southern hill of Mount Zhong 15 kilometers west of the seat of Zichang County. It was built in the fourth year (1067) of the Zhiping reign of the Song Dynasty. Inside the cave there are three sizable statues and more than 10,000 varied, life-like ones. The bigger ones, 3.5 meters in height, represent Kasyapa, Sakyamuni and Maitreya respectively. These statues, though centuries old, still keep the original colors of paint. There are many stone tablets both in and out of the cave. Among the well-preserved relics are the Memorial Archway, the Xiaoci Hall, Master Hui Shan's stupa, Master Song Yan's stupa, the seven-story brick pagoda, and the Meditation Room. Mount Zhongshan Cave is now a class-A historical monument under the sate protection.

▲ "自在觀音"
The Goddess of Mercy at Ease

石窟一隅
▼ A Partial View of the Grottoes

▲ 菩薩群像　A Gathering of Buddhisattvas

▲ 釋迦车尼造像　A Statue of Sakyamuni

▼ 十菩薩造像　A Statue Complex of Ten Buddisattvas

# 紅石峽　The Red Rock Canyon

紅石峽位於榆林市城北3公里處，兩邊懸崖對峙，榆溪河穿峽而過。夕陽西照，紅石映日，分外耀目。崖壁上有明清以來開鑿的洞窟廟堂44處，以"天門"、"石階"隧洞相通。峽壁上留有160余幅歷代名人的題刻。是珍貴的書法寶庫。

The Red Rock Canyon is located three kilometers north of Yulin City. Between its precipitous cliffs on both sides is flowing a river named Yuxi River. At sunset, its cliff rocks are a mass of shining redness. About 44 caves were dug into its cliffs in the Ming and Qing dynasties. These caves are accessible the visiting public by following the stone steps through the Skyward Gate. There are many literary men's inscriptions on the surfaces of the cliffs. The inscriptions constitute an important part of the treasure house of the Chinese calligraphy.

▲ 石窟及石刻
The Stone Cave & its Inscriptions

紅石峽風光
▼ The Red Rock Canyon in Splendor

▲ 中部石窟　　The Grottoes in the Central Area

▼ 北部石窟　　The Grottoes in the Northern Area

# 鎮北臺　Zhenbeitai Beacon Tower

鎮北臺位於榆林市城北5公里的紅山上，建于明萬歷35年（公元1607年），是長城最大的烽火臺。臺爲正方形，共4層，外砌磚石，體積逐層遞減，佔地近5000平方米，總高約30米。臺的第一層環列駐軍營房。登臺遠眺，塞內、塞外景色一覽無餘。爲省重點文物保護單位。

Zhenbeitai Beacon Tower, which is located on the Red Hill five kilometers north of Yulin City, was built in the thirty-fifth year (1607) of the Wanli reign of the Ming Dynasty. It is the most sizable beacon tower on the Great Wall. The tower is square, four-storied, and veneered with bricks. Its circumference decreases from one storey to another. The tower is 5,000 square meters in size, and approximately 30 meters in height. The first story was initially used as military barracks At the top of the tower, one can take a bird's view of the scenes north and south of the Great Wall. Zhenbeitai Beacon Tower is now a class-A historical monument under the provincial protection.

▲ 鎮北臺周圍的長城
The Great Wall Around the Beacon Tower

鎮北臺
▼ Zhenbeitai Beacon Tower

# 毛烏素沙漠 Mu Us Desert

毛烏素沙漠是我國第四大沙漠，東起榆林，西至內蒙古的鄂托克前旗，長約400公里，寬12－120公里。較佳的觀景點是榆林市西約60公里的補浪河鄉。這裏沙質細膩，沙丘高約10－30米，隨着風向、風力及地勢的變化，沙漠的形態也隨之變幻。或沙丘橫亙，跌宕起伏；或微波細紋，婀娜多姿。若再走入沙丘的灘地，還會看到星羅棋布的海子，"大漠孤煙直，長河落日圓"的景象便會展現在您眼前。間或點綴的沙漠植物及小動物還可能帶給您意外的驚喜。

Mu Us Desert, the 4th largest desert in China, stretches for about 400 kilometers from Yulin City in the east to Inner Mongolia's Otog Front Banner in the west. It ranges in width from 12 to 120 kilometers. The generally-accepted point of view is located in Bulianghe Town, about 60 kilometers west of Yulin City. Its sand is fine in size. Its dunes range in height from 10 to 30 meters, and constantly vary in shape with wind-force, wind directions and terrains. They rise and fall irregularly, and provide a gripping view. Noticeably, Mu Us Desert is endowed with oases and lakes among its sand dunes. When you travel there, you will not fail to feast your eyes on the beauty of rising smoke and beautiful sunset scenes, and see plants and animals on the desert.

浩瀚的毛烏素
▼ The Vast Expanse of Mu Us Desert

▲  大漠暢想曲  魯少河攝  The Inspiring Desert  (Photo by Lu Shao-he)

▲ 沙漠的紋理
The Grains of the Desert

▲ 沙漠游人
Desert Travelers

◀ 秋季的沙漠
The Autumn Scene in the
Desert

沙漠驕子　　　▶
The Blessed in the Desert

　▲ 沙漠邊的海子　　The Lake on the Rim of the Desert

毛烏素沙漠至大夏統萬城的沿途景色
The Site of the Xia Dynasty's Tongwan City

# 大夏統萬城
## The Ruins of the Xia Dynasty's Tongwan City

統萬城是沙漠中的一座城池，位於靖邊縣紅墩界鄉北邊。是大夏國國君赫連勃勃於公元413年歷時5年，招募10萬民夫用蒸土拌畜血修築而成。後宋太宗明令予以毀棄，移民20萬至銀、綏二州，從此，有600年歷史的統萬城逐漸變爲廢墟。現在遺址上仍可見東城、西城和廓城三部分。

Tongwan City, a centuries-old settlement in the desert, is located in the north of Hongduijie Town, Jingbian County. The city was built with a mixture of steamed soil and animal blood in the year of 413 when King Helinberb ruled over the Xia Empire. It took 100,000 laborers 5 years to bring the city into completion. When it came to the Song Dynasty, Emperor Tai Zong gave orders to raze the city and move 200,000 people to the Yin and Sui districts there. As a result, the 600-year-old Tongwan city was ruined. Nevertheless, the East City, the West City and the Outer City are still identifiable today.

▲ 西南角樓遺跡
The Site of the Southwest Corner Tower

南城垣及敵臺遺跡
▼ The Sites of the South City Wall and the Rampart

# 二 郎 山 廟 宇
## Erlangshan Temple

一郎山位於神木縣城西0.5公里的窟野河、芹河交匯處，因上有二郎廟得名。此山呈南北走向，雙峰兀起，中稍低凹，山勢陡峭，直刺雲天，儼然一道天然屏障。400多年前順着蜿蜒起伏的山脊修建的近百座殿、廟、亭、閣，古朴而玄妙，形成了少有的奇特景觀。爲省重點文物保護單位。

Erlangshan Temple stands at the intersection of Kuye and Qinhe rivers 0.5 kilometer west of Shenmu County. Initially, it was named for Erlang Temple. The mountain stretches from north to south, with two prominent peaks, and provides a natural protective screen for the seat of Shenmu County. Approximately 400 years ago, halls, temples, pavilions and towers were built along its wave-like ridge. These structures are simple and unsophisticated, and afford a unique delight to visitors.

▲ 懸崖上的神龕
The Cliffside Niche

仰望二郎山廟
▼ A View of Mt Erlang Temple

▲ 鳥瞰大雄寶殿、娘娘廟等廟宇　　The Hall of Mahavira and the Temple of the Goddess of Fertility

# 紅 鹼 淖　The Red Alkali Lake

　　**紅**鹼淖位於神木縣70公里處的爾林兔鎮，是陝西省最大的天然湖泊。因此地富含紅鹼，地面呈鐵銹色而得名。

　　湖面約6670公頃，平均水深15米，煙波浩淼，碧波粼粼。此湖四面環沙，沙柳遍地。湖東南方有絨毯般的大草原，各色野花點綴其間。每年3－4月及10－12月還有大量的天鵝、大雁、鷺鷥等候鳥遷途至此，給靜謐的湖區平添了幾分生氣。因水質關系，魚蝦味道鮮美異常。

　　紅鹼淖原始風貌保持良好，是融湖泊、沙灘、草原為一體的省級風景區。

The Red Alkali Lake, which is located in Erlintu Town 70 kilometers north of the seat of Shenmu County, is the largest natural lake in Shaanxi Province. The lake was named for its alkali-rich water and the red soil around.

About 6,670 hectares in area and 15 meters in depth, the lake is a vast expanse of misty, rolling waters, embraced by sands. There are willow trees everywhere. To the southeast of the lake lies a vast stretch of velvety grassland dotted with wild flowers. Vast numbers of birds, such as white swans, wild geese and egrets, make it their temporary home from March to April and from October to December every year, thus bringing much life and vituality, the lake produces very delicious fish and shrimps.

The Red Alkali Lake is well-preserved in terms of its primitive traits. It is an attractive travel destination in Shaanxi Province, which affords a vast view of lake, desert and grassland scenes.

▲ 紅鹼淖
A View of The Red Alkali Lake

紅鹼淖鳥群
▼ The Migratory Birds in the Area of the Lake

# 白雲山道觀　Mount Baiyun Temple

素稱"關西名勝"的白雲觀位於佳縣城南、黃河之濱的白雲山上。始建於明萬曆33年（公元1605年）。共有廟宇53座，建築面積達81000平方米，是明清時期西北最大的古建築群和道教聖地。現存彩色壁畫1900餘幅，各代碑碣108塊，匾額40餘塊以及石獅、古鐘、浮雕、石刻等珍貴文物。為省重點文物保護單位。一年三次的古廟會（即農曆三月三、四月八、九月九），吸引着陝、甘、寧、晉、蒙等地各族民衆蜂擁而至。

Mount Baiyun Temple, which is known as a famous place of historical interest to the west of the Hangu Pass, is located on Mount Baiyuan by the side of the Yellow River to the south of Jiaxian County. The temple was initially built in the 33-rd year (1605) of the Wanli reign of the Ming Dynasty. This sacred place is dotted with 53 Taoist temples, with a total floor space of 81,000 square meters. The building complex was the most sizable in the northwest region of the and Qing dynasties. There are more than 1,900 painted mural paintings, 108 steles, over 40 horizontal inscribed boards, stone lions, ancient iron bells, relief sculptures and stone carvings all over the mountain. Mount Baiyun Temple is now orical monument under the provincial protection. The temple fair, which is held three times a year, attracts vast numbers of people from Shaanxi, Gansu, Ningxia, Shan and Inner Mongolia.

▲ "登雲梯"
The Skyward Ladder

◀ 玉皇閣
The Jade Emperor's Pavilion

▲ 黃河岸邊的白雲觀　　Mount Baiyun Temple by the Yellow River

▼ 眞武大殿院　　The Hall of the God of Northern Lunar Mansions

# 香爐寺　Xianglu Temple

香爐寺位於佳縣城東北1公里的香爐峰頂，創建於明萬曆十一年（1583）。東臨黃河，三面空絕，僅西北一狹徑與城相通。峰前有直徑5米，高20餘米的的巨石兀立，形似高足香爐。它與寺院間懸一"斷橋"相連。頂端建有觀音樓，登臨俯瞰，但見河水奔騰猶如凌絕空際。毛澤東曾到此游覽。

Xianglu Temple, which is located at the top of the Xianglu Peak one kilometer northeast of the seat of Jiaxian County, took shape in the eleventh year (1583) of the Wanli reign of the Ming Dynasty. The peak looks over the Yellow River in the east, and exposes steep cliffs on the other three sides. There is a narrow path in the northwest of the peak that leads to the county seat. A huge stone, 5 in diameter and over 20 meters in height, stands in front of the peak The stone is shaped like a high-legged incense burner, and connected with the temple by a "broken suspense bridge". When you get to the Chamber of Avalokitesvara and look afar, you will see the mighty waters of the Yellow River rolling on incessantly temple  during his stay in north Shaanxi.

# 李自成行宫　Li Zi-cheng's Resort Palace

李自成行宫座落在米脂縣城北盤龍山南麓。1643年李自成率義軍回師陝北駐於此地。"行宫"主體由樂樓、梅花亭、捧聖樓、二天門、玉皇閣、啓祥殿、兆慶宫等7處主要建築組成。前有無定河迴繞，后有群山環抱，龍盤虎踞，氣勢雄偉，是黄土高原上保存完整的明代古建築群。

Li Zi-cheng's Resort Palace is located on the southern hill of Mount Panlong north of the seat of Mizi County in northern Shaanxi, where Li Zi-cheng stationed his revolt army in 1943. The palace consists of the Music Chamber, the Plum Blossom Pavilion, the Imperial Chamber, the Ertianmen Gate, the Jade Emperor Chamber, the Qixiang Hall and the Zhaoqing Hall. The palace looks over the winding Yongding River in front, and stands against green hills on the other three sides. This splendid architectural complex is the best preserved Ming-dynasty structure on the Loess Plateau.

▲ 捧聖樓　The Pengsheng Tower

▲ 行宮全貌　　A Panorama of the Resort Palace

▼ 攬勝樓　　The Lansheng Tower

# 壺口瀑布
## Hukou Waterfall

壺口瀑布位於宜川縣與山西吉縣交界處，是我國第二大瀑布。

相傳爲大禹治水勝跡。當滾滾黃河流經此處時，河面由近300米突然緊束爲約50米寬，飛奔直瀉，落入30多米下的河漕，宛如自壺嘴倒出。濤聲如雷，霧氣彌漫。以其排山倒海的雄渾氣勢而名震天下；以其象徵和代表着中華民族文化精髓而爲炎黃子孫所向往。是國家重點風景名勝區。

Hukou Waterfall, the second largest waterfall in China, is located at the juncture of Yichuan County in Shaanxi Province and Jixian County in Shanxi Province. Legend has it that the phenomenon resulted from Da Yu's endeavors to bring the Yellow River under control. At the point, the river abruptly narrows its course from 300 to 50 meters, dashes down the 30-meter precipice into a trough, and then pours out of the trough with mighty power, thus producing a misty and overhanging waterfall. Its mier symbolizes the quintessence of the Chinese culture and the aspirations of the Chinese people. Hukou Waterfall is now a scenic attraction under the priority protection of the state government.

▲ 千里黃河一壺收　　The Yellow River at the Hukou Waterfall

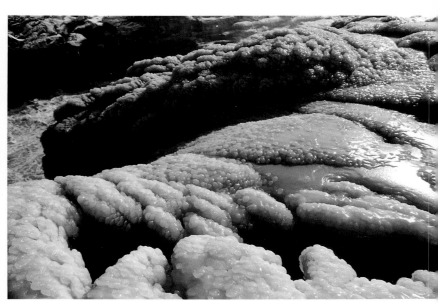

▶ 橫跨壺口表演
The Performance of Crossing Hukou Waterfall

▲ 壺口冬景　李靜攝
The Winter Scene at Hukou Waterfall (Photo by Li Jing)

壺口瀑布　王沛攝
▼ Hukou Waterfall　(Photo by Wang Pei)

▲ 10里龍槽
The 10-Mile Dragon Trough

仰望壺口　秦小平攝
▼ An Upward View of Hukou Waterfall（Photo by Qin Xiao-ping）

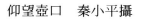

▲ 水
T

▲ 俯視壺口　　A Bird's Eye View of Hukou Waterfall

宜川城東南的"老虎梁"景色
▼ A Scene of the Tiger Ridge Southeast of Yichuan County

状地貌
er-eroded, Jar-shaped Land Forms

▲ 沿途經過的宜川英旺川景色　　The Scene at Yingwang Chuan in Yichuan County

▲ 原始禮花 " 打花 "
The Conventional Fireworks

◀ 嗩吶
The Suona Musical Instrument

民間祭品
▼ The Sacrificial Offerings in Northern Shaanxi

男子腰鼓
The Men's Waist Drum

▲ 女子腰鼓　謝妮婭攝　　The Women's Waist Drum (Photo by Xie Ni-ya)

▼ 趕集　　At the Town Fair

貓和蝴蝶（剪紙） 李秀芳作
Papercut Work: A Cat and
Butterflies (By Li Xiu-fang)

大公雞（農民畫） 曹佃祥作
Peasant Painting: The
▼ Cock （By Cao Dian-xiang)

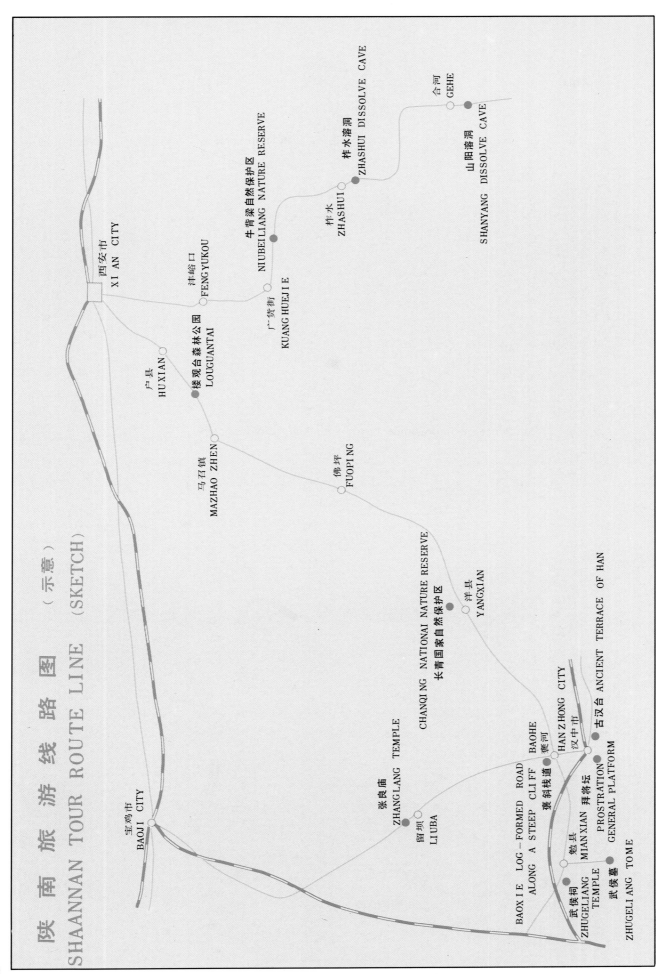

陕 南 旅 游 线 路 图 （示意）
SHAANNAN TOUR ROUTE LINE (SKETCH)

西安市 XI AN CITY

祚水溶洞 ZHASHUI DISSOLVE CAVE

合河 GEHE

山阳溶洞 SHANYANG DISSOLVE CAVE

牛背梁自然保护区 NIUBEILIANG NATURE RESERVE

祚水 ZHASHUI

拜峪口 FENGYUKOU

广货街 KUANG HUEJIE

户县 HUXIAN

楼观台森林公园 LOUGUANTAI

马召镇 MAZHAO ZHEN

佛坪 FUOPING

长青国家自然保护区 CHANQING NATIONAI NATURE RESERVE

洋县 YANGXIAN

古汉台 ANCIENT TERRACE OF HAN

汉中市 HAN ZHONG CITY

褒河 BAOHE

宝鸡市 BAOJI CITY

张良庙 ZHANG LANG TEMPLE

留坝 LIUBA

褒斜栈道 BAOXIE LOG–FORMED ROAD ALONG A STEEP CLIFF

勉县 MIANXIAN

拜将坛 PROSTRATION GENERAL PLATFORM

武侯祠 ZHUGELIANG TEMPLE

武侯墓 ZHUGELIANG TOME

# 褒斜棧道　Baoxie Plank Road

褒斜棧道是橫跨秦嶺連接漢中關中鑿石架木而成的古要道。建於秦惠文王時（前337年——前311年），是我國歷史上開鑿最早、規模最大的棧道。為國家重點文物保護單位。它南起漢中褒河谷口，經留壩縣、太白縣，北至眉縣斜峪關，總長500公里。前316年，秦派兵伐蜀通過此道。自此，該道一直是南北兵家往來必爭之路。三國時期，諸葛亮北攻曹魏，後兵敗退回漢中均經此道。今古道多已毀損，但殘跡尚存。其氣勢從漢中西北約15公里處的褒河谷修複棧道可窺見一斑。

Baoxie Plank Road which was built during King Huiwenwang's Reign (337 B.C.--311 B.C.) of the Qin State provided a link of communication over the Qinling Range between Hanzhong District and the Central Shaanxi Plains in the ancient times. The first and longest of its kind in history, Baoxie Plank Road is now placed under the state's priority protection. It starts from the mouth of the Baohe River Valley in the city of Hanzhong, cuts through Liuba Countys to Xieyu Pass. The road covers a total distance of 500 kilometers. It is the road that the Qin army followed on its expedition against the Shu Kingdom in 316 B.C. The road used to be of strategic importance for the ancient sovereign states. During today. The visitor can obtain a general picture of the plan k road from the restored section along the Baohe River Valley about 15 kilometers northwest of Hanzhou City.

▲ 棧道上面的情景
On the Plank Road

遠眺褒斜道
▼ A Distant View of the Plank Road

# 張良廟　Zhang Liang's Temple

張良廟位於留壩縣城北15公里的紫柏山下。於東漢末年爲紀念西漢三傑之一的著名政治家張良所建。有大小9院，156間房舍，面積1.42萬平方米。主要建築有張良大殿、三清殿、靈官殿、授書樓等。樓閣亭園建築風格融南方園林式和北方宮殿式爲一體，靈秀而壯觀。廟外五山合抱，滿目紫柏；二水夾流，溪聲淙淙；加之雲飄霧繞，恍若仙境。爲省重點文物保護單位。與紫柏山共同構成集觀光、度假、避暑、科研爲一體的旅游區，是省風景名勝區。

Zhang Liang's Temple which is located at the foot of Mount Zibo fifteen kilometers north of the seat of Liuba County, was built in the closing years of the Eastern Han Dynasty in memory of Zhang Liang, one of the three most famous politicians. With 9 courtyards and 156 partitioned rooms, the temple covers an area of 14,200 square meters. Its major building structures are the Great Hall of Zhang Liang, the Sanqing Hall, the Lingguan Hall, and the Shoushu Chamber. In architectural style, it combines southern garden-type structures with northern palatial buildings. The entire architectural complex is magnificent and inspiring. The temple is embraced by hills with a dense covering of pine trees, and surrounded by two babbling rivers. It is enveloped in clouds of mist just like a blessed paradise. Up to date, the whole area has been well-planned to serve the various needs of sightseers, holiday-makers and researchers. It is now a scenic resort of historical interest under the priority protection of the provincial government.

▲ 二山門
The Ershan Gate

北花園
▼ The North Garden

授書樓
The Shoushu Chamber

▲ 靈官殿　The Lingguan Hall

# 武侯祠 Wuhou's Temple

武侯祠位於勉縣城西3公里川陝公路的南沿、漢江以北，于蜀漢景耀六年（公元263年）爲紀念諸葛亮，蜀后主劉禪下詔在武侯坪所建，明正德八年（公元1513年）遷於此地。共占地2.27公頃，殿廡、游廊、房舍70餘間，主要有大殿、拜殿、琴樓、樂樓、戟門等建築。現存石碑59通。祠內古柏參天、旱蓮丹桂相映成趣，環境幽雅寂靜。是省重點文物保護單位。

Wuhou Temple, which is located south of Sichuan-Shaanxi High way three kilometers west of the seat of Mianxian County, was initially built by Liu Chan's imperial orders on the Wuhou Tableland in the sixth year (263 A.D.) of the Jingyao reign in memory of Zhuge Liang, a well-known strategist of the Shu Kingdom. It was relocated to the present-day site in the eighth year (1513) of the Zhengde reign of the Ming Dynasty. The temple covers an area of 2.27 hectares. It primarily consists of the Great Hall, the Sacrificial Hall, the Harp Chamber, the Music Chamber and winding corridors. Within its precincts stand 59 stone tablets and centuries-old towering pine trees. The heady fragrance of orange osmanthus and Camptotheca acuminata wafts through the air. With a quiet and elegant environment, Wuhou's Temple is now a class-A historical monument under the provincial protection.

拜殿外景
▼ The Exterior of the Memorial Hall

▲ 鼓楼
The Drum Tower

"天下第一流"牌楼
▼ The "World's Number One" A

◀ 琴楼
The Harp-playing Chamber

120

▲ 樂樓
The Music Chamber

祠內一角
▼ A View of the Temple

# 古漢臺　The Ancient Han Dynasty Platform

古漢臺位於漢中市內，是漢劉邦的宮廷遺址。臺高8米，面積7000多平方米。周圍臺垣高聳，有望江樓等建築。爲省重點文物保護單位。漢臺現爲漢中市博物館館址，內辟有"石門十三品陳列館"和"褒斜棧道史陳列館。"在其它陳列館還珍藏着出土文物千餘件及許多歷史名人字畫、題記、石刻等。

The Ancient Han Dynasty Platform, located within the city of Hanzhong, marks the site of Emperor Liu Bang's imperial palace. The platform is 8 meters in height and over 7,000 square meters in size. Worthy of notice is the Riverside Watch Tower within its precincts. The platform marks the location of Hanzhong Municipal History Museum, with exhibitions on the locally-unearthed relics and the history of Baoxie Plank Road. The museum houses more than 1,000 articles of historical value, paintings, calligraphic works, stone inscriptions and carvings. The platform is now a historical monument under the priority protection of the provincial government.

▲ 漢台大門
The Front Gate to the Palace

庭院建築一角
▼ A Partial View of the Building Complex

望江樓建築局部
A Partial View of the Riverside Tower

望江樓
▼ The Riverside Tower

# 拜 將 壇
## The Military Post Assignment Platform

拜將壇位於漢中市南。是公元前206年劉邦拜韓信爲大將，於此設壇舉行儀式的遺址。面積7,840平方米。臺北有亭閣一座，南有"漢大將韓信拜將壇"石碑一通。

The Military Post Assignment Platform which is located in the south of Hanzhong City is where Han Dynasty Emperor Liu Bang ceremonially appointed Han Xin chief military general in 206 B.C.. The platform covers an area of 7,840 square meters. There stand a pavilion in the north and a stone tablet in the south. The tablet was inscribed with a brief description of the military post assignment event.

▲ 拜將壇遺址
The Site of the Military Post Assignment Platform

# 長青國家自然保護區
## The Evergreen National Natural Reserve

長青自然保護區位於洋縣城北65公里處的秦嶺中段南坡，總面積3萬公頃。該區處於南北植物交匯地帶及動物地理上的古北界和東洋界交匯處，動植物種類繁多。有喬本植物72種、灌木50多種，竹類主要爲巴山木竹和松花竹。有國家一級保護動物大熊貓、金絲猴、羚牛，國家二級保護動物黑熊、血雉、林麝等共25種，其中大熊貓有80餘只，約占秦嶺大熊貓總數的1/3。

保護區內風景秀麗，鳥語花香，實爲一塊難得的"淨土"。

The Evergreen National Natural Reserve lies on the southern slope of the central Qinling Range 65 kilometers north of Yangxian County, and covers a total area of 30,000 hectares.

The natural reserve, which lies in the transitional region for northern and southern plants, and also for palearctic and oriental animals, is an optimum habitat for a great variety of plants and animals. Its vegetation mainly includes seventy-two arbor pecies, more than fifty shrub species, Bashan bamboo and Songhua bamboo. Among its animal resources are the class-A state-protected animals: the golden-haired monkey and the antelope; and the class-B state-protected animals: the black bear and the Ithaginis cruentus. Across the reserve there are more than 80 giant pandas, roughly 1/3 of the total number on the Qinling Range.

With a quiet and beautiful environment, the reserve is rated as a land "high purity".

▲ 科研人員與熊貓　張廣良攝
The Researchers and the Giant Panda
(Photo by Zhang Guang-liang )

天然次生林
▼ The Natural Secondary Forest

保護區內的大熊貓　此組照片　張廣良攝
The Giant Pandas in the Natural Reserve
(Photo by Zhang Guang-liang)

# 榨水溶洞
## The Limestone Caves in Zhashui County

▲ 溶洞外景"對峰臺"
The Double Peak Platform
Outside the Cave

二佛觀海市
▼ Two Buddhas Are Watching
the Mirage

榨水溶洞位於秦嶺南麓榨水縣的石甕鄉，北距西安147公里。是以溶洞爲主，山水風光爲輔的自然景區。

此地山體爲喀斯特地貌。100多個大小不一的溶洞形成了龐大的溶洞群，洞內鐘乳石形態各異。現已開發3個溶洞。佛爺洞屬廳堂式溶洞，有"二佛觀海市"、"蘑菇塔"、"水帘洞"等景。天洞爲廊道式溶洞，"玉瀑廳"、"蓮花池"、"龍宮"爲主要景觀。風洞是廳堂與廊道兼有的溶洞。"東海波濤"、"龍女出海"等景栩栩如生。

這里山青水秀，風光旖旎，夏季避暑甚佳。

The limestone caves are located in Shiweng Town, Zhashui County in the southern hill of the Qinling Range. The scenic area, which is 147 kilometers away from the city of Xi'an, takes limestone caves and beautiful scenery as a combined whole.

This mountainous region is characterized by its Karst land forms. The limestone caves, more than 1,000 in number and varied in size, constitute a large-sized complex of Karst caves. The stalactite inside the caves are bizarrely shaped. Up to date, three of the caves have been opened to the visiting public. The Cave of the Buddhas comprises such sights as the Two Buddhas Watching the Mirage, the Mushroom Tower, and the Waterfall Cave. The Cave of the Heaven consists of the Jade Waterfall Hall, the Lotus Pond and the Dragon Palace. The Windy Cave is made of the East Sea Waves and the Dragon Lady at Sea.

The scenic area is embraced by green hills and clear waters. It affords a welcome break from summer heat.

磨菇塔
The Mushroom Tower

▼ 水帘洞景色　The Waterfall Cave

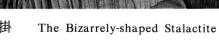

▲ 奇妙的鐘乳石壁掛　The Bizarrely-shaped Stalactite

前往溶洞途經的樺水牛背梁自然保護區
The Natural Preserve on the Niubei Ridge

▼ 沿途的山花　　The Mountain Flowers en Route

▲ 沿途的小溪　　The Stream en Route

▲ 保護區秋色　　The Autumn Scene of the Natural Reserve

▼ 通往榨水溶洞的公路　　The Highway Leading to Zhashui Limestone Caves

# 山陽溶洞　The Limestone Cave in Shanyang

山陽溶洞（亦稱月亮洞）位於山陽縣城西南55公里處的合河鄉，該溶洞全長1000多米，內有大量彩色鐘乳石。有的似磨菇，有的象羅漢，有的則宛如傳說中的龍門……洞內還栖息着大量的蝙蝠。

Shanyang Limestone Cave or the Moon Cave is located in Hehe Town 55 kilometers west of the seat of Shanyang County. The cave, more than 1,000 meters in length, has plenty of colored stalactite inside it. The stalactite is shaped like the mushroom, the legendary Dragon Gate or the arbot. Inside the cave there live a large number of bats.

山陽溶洞一瞥
A Snapshot of the Limestone Cave

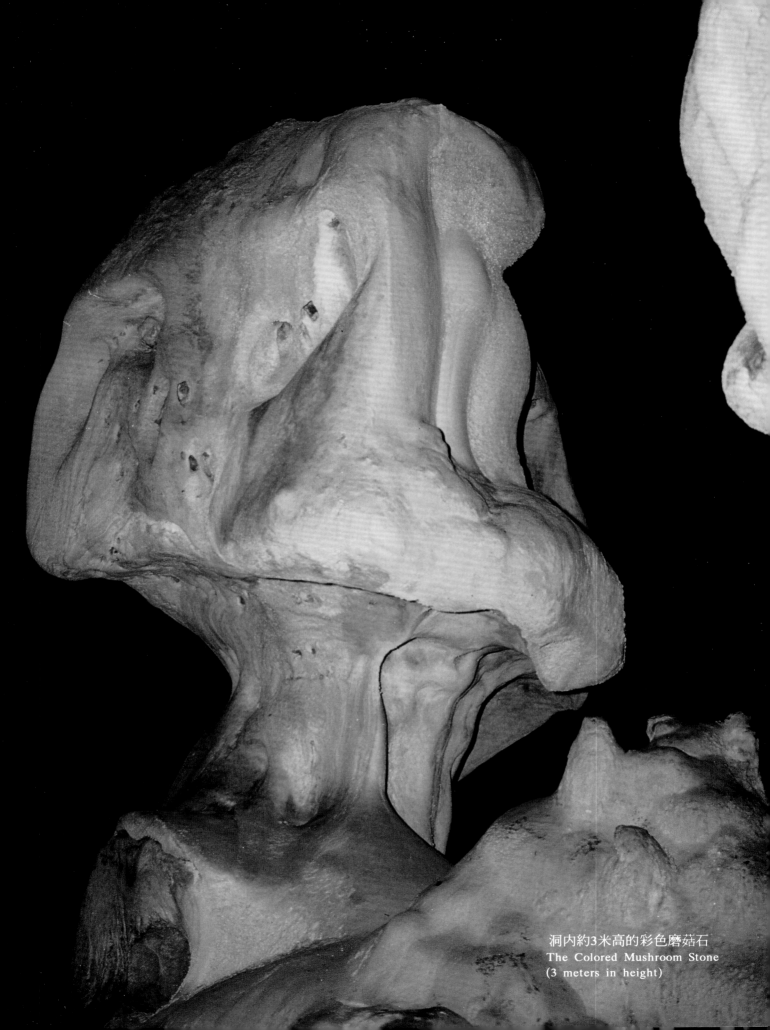

洞内約3米高的彩色磨菇石
The Colored Mushroom Stone
(3 meters in height)

▲ 芯子
The Theatrical Performance in the Air

▲ 吊鍋
The Hanging Pot

出山
▼ Taking a Trip Beyond the M[o

138

▼ 牧鴨
Herding Ducks

▲ 小橋流水人家
The Bridge, the River and the
Residential Dwelling

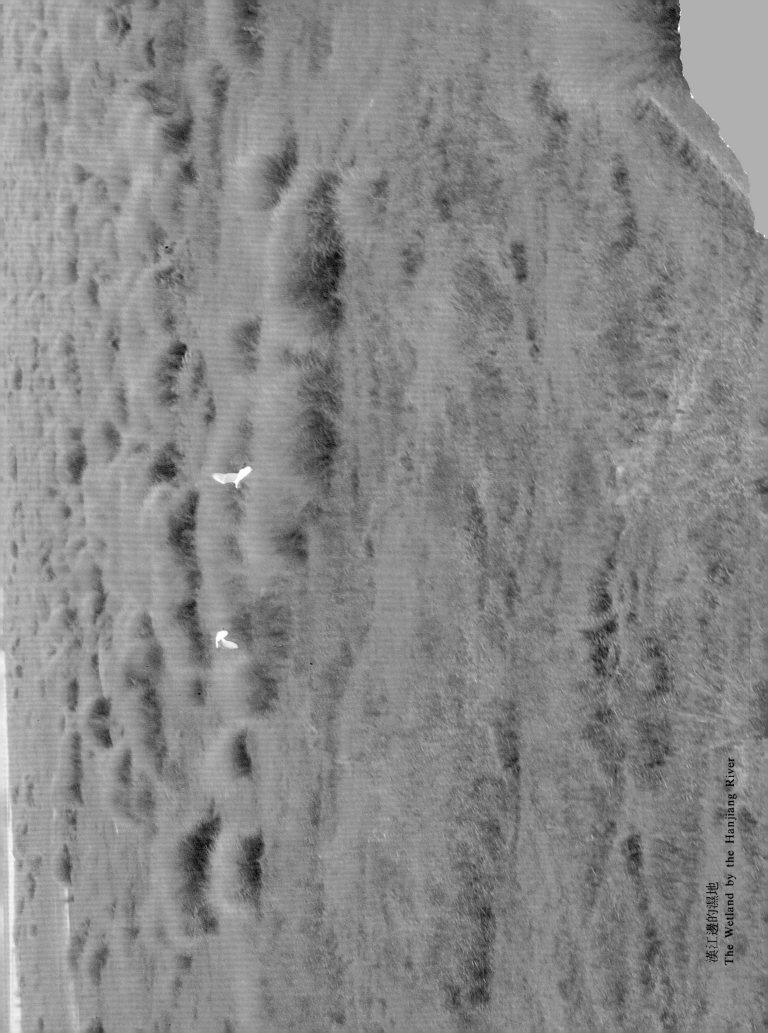

漢江邊的濕地
The Wetland by the Hanjiang River